THIS BOOK BELONGS TO:

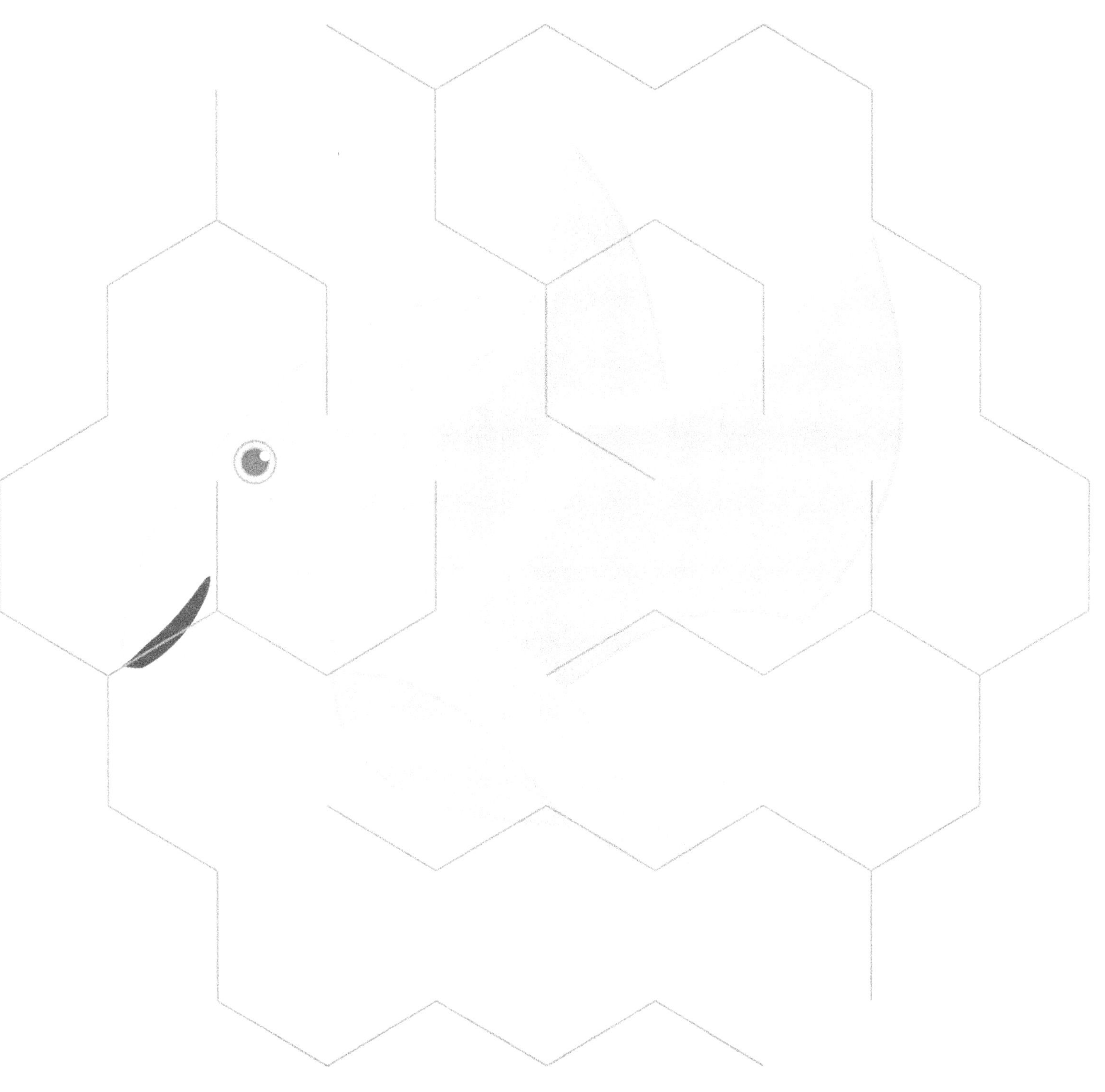

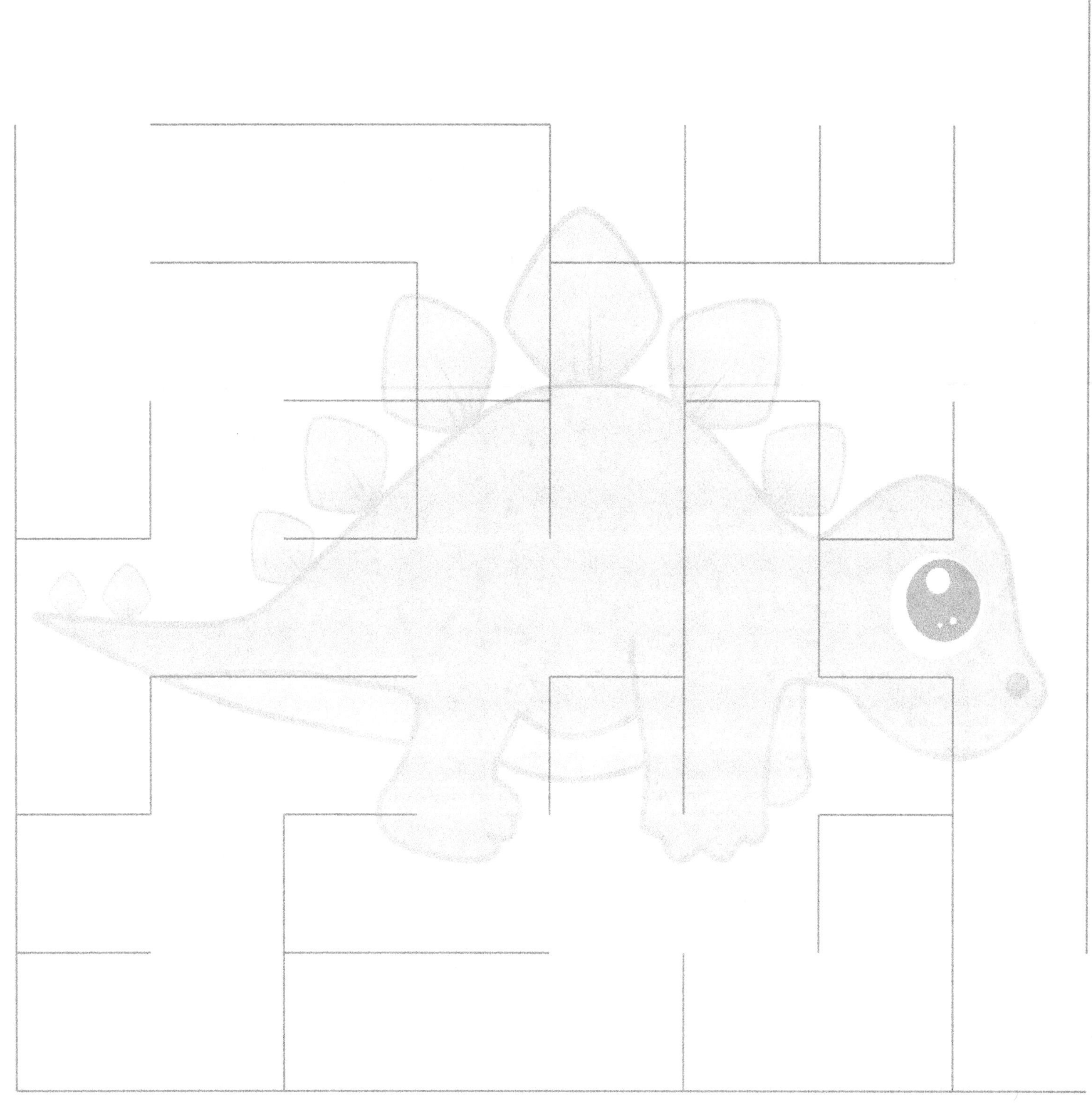

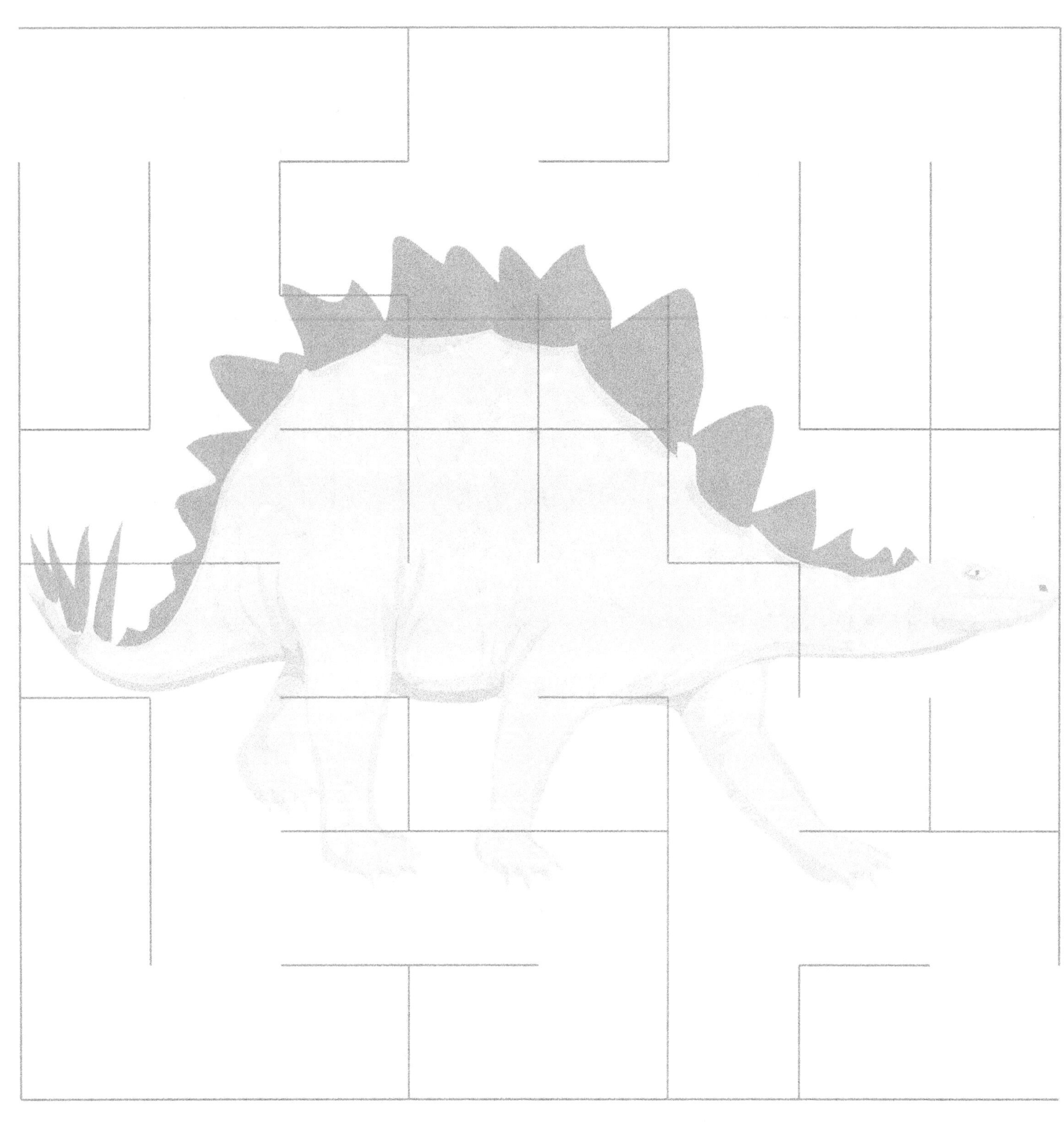

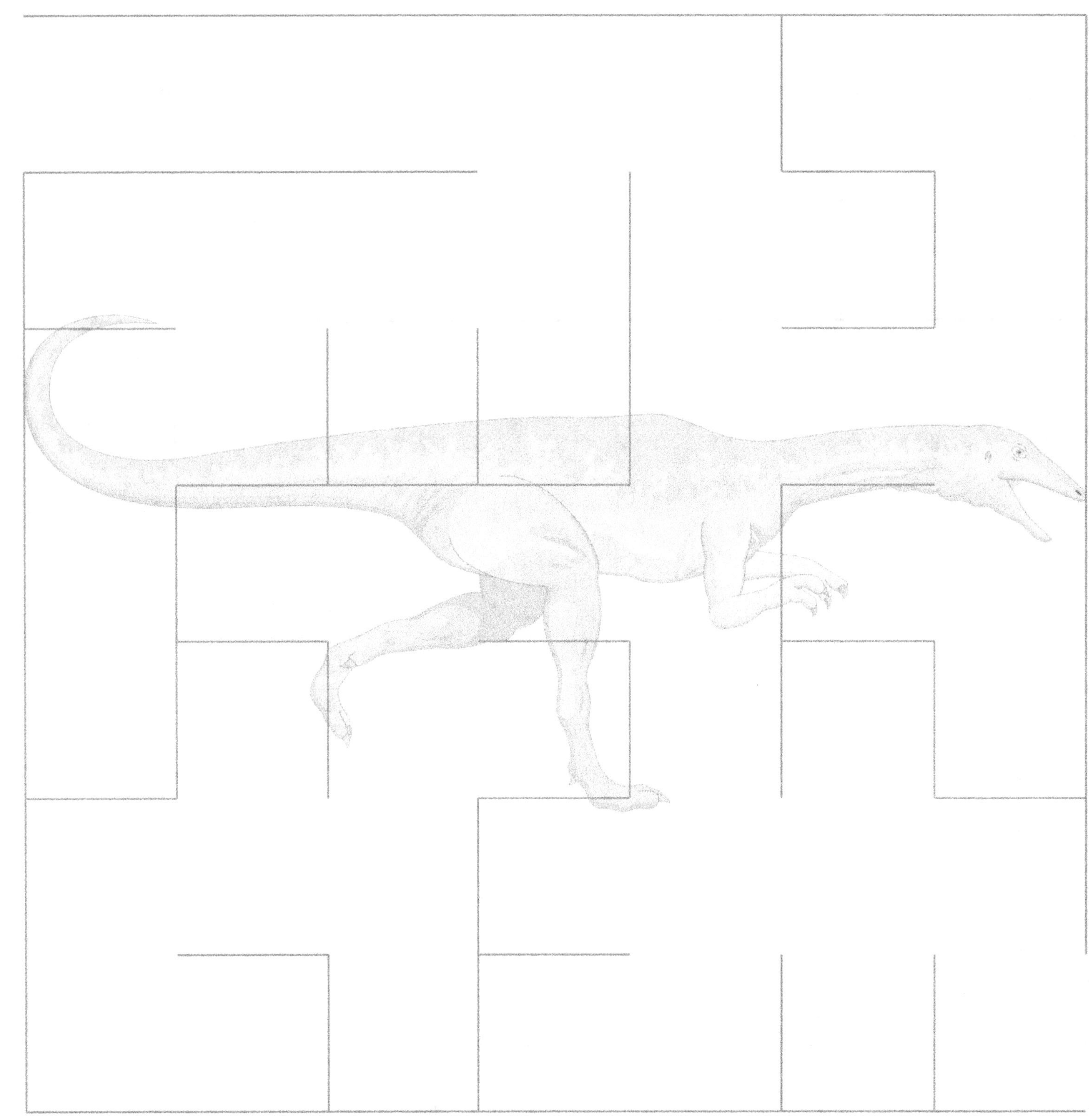

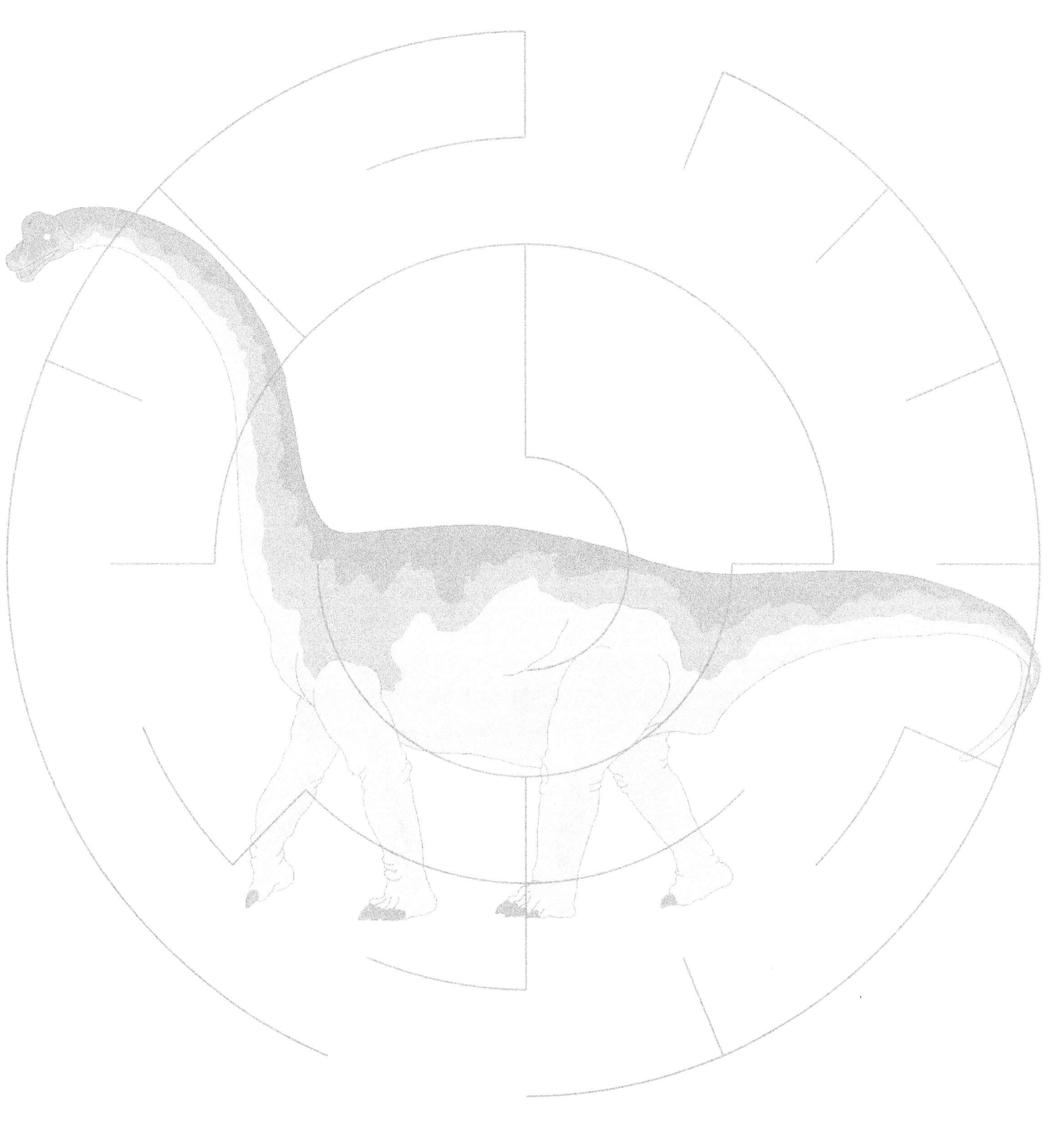